Dear Parent:
Your child's love of reading starts here!

Every child learns to read in a different way and at his or her own speed. Some go back and forth between reading levels and read favorite books again and again. Others read through each level in order. You can help your young reader improve and become more confident by encouraging his or her own interests and abilities. From books your child reads with you to the first books he or she reads alone, there are I Can Read Books for every stage of reading:

SHARED READING
Basic language, word repetition, and whimsical illustrations, ideal for sharing with your emergent reader

BEGINNING READING
Short sentences, familiar words, and simple concepts for children eager to read on their own

READING WITH HELP
Engaging stories, longer sentences, and language play for developing readers

READING ALONE
Complex plots, challenging vocabulary, and high-interest topics for the independent reader

ADVANCED READING
Short paragraphs, chapters, and exciting themes for the perfect bridge to chapter books

I Can Read Books have introduced children to the joy of reading since 1957. Featuring award-winning authors and illustrators and a fabulous cast of beloved characters, I Can Read Books set the standard for beginning readers.

A lifetime of discovery begins with the magical words **"I Can Read!"**

Visit www.icanread.com for information
on enriching your child's reading experience.

To Emma
—D.G.

To Lisa, Cam, and Rosie
—J.P.

*The author gratefully acknowledges the editorial
contributions of Lori Houran.*

I Can Read Book® is a trademark of HarperCollins Publishers.

My Weird School: Class Pet Mess! Text copyright © 2017 by Dan Gutman. Illustrations copyright © 2017 by Jim Paillot. All rights reserved. Manufactured in U.S.A. No part of this book may be used or reproduced in any manner whatsoever without written permission except in the case of brief quotations embodied in critical articles and reviews. For information address HarperCollins Children's Books, a division of HarperCollins Publishers, 195 Broadway, New York, NY 10007.
www.icanread.com

ISBN 978-0-06-236746-4 (pbk. bdg.)—ISBN 978-0-06-2367474-1 (hardcover)

I Can Read!

READING 2 WITH HELP

My WeiRd School

Class Pet Mess!

Dan Gutman
Pictures by Jim Paillot

HARPER
An Imprint of HarperCollinsPublishers

My name is Alexia

and I hate bunnies.

Well, not really.

But I don't want one

for a class pet.

Why?

Because Andrea *does*.

"A fluffy little bunny would be
so cute!" she said on Friday.
"*So* cute," agreed Emily.
Emily always agrees with Andrea.
It's totally annoying.

"I think we should get
something *cool*," I said.
"Like a snake."
"YEAH!" said all the boys.

"EW!" said all the girls.

Mr. Cooper let us vote.

Lucky for me, there are

more boys than girls in the class.

"No fair!" whined Andrea.

"Tough luck," A.J. said.

"Hey, Mr. Cooper, can we get a *poisonous* snake?"

He looked right at Andrea.

"No special reason."

"Fat chance," said Mr. Cooper.

Oh well.

Even a regular snake beats a bunny.

On Monday, Mr. Cooper

brought in a tank.

Coiled up inside was a snake!

"This is an eastern hognose.

His name is Bob."

Then Mr. Cooper announced

that since the snake was my idea,

I got to feed Bob the first week!

"He mostly eats live toads,"

Mr. Cooper said.

"Gross!" said Andrea, covering her ears.

"Gross!" I said, clapping my hands.

This was going to be awesome!

Mr. Cooper told the class more stuff about hognose snakes.

Their habitats, their defenses, blah blah blah.

All I cared about was the toad part.

I couldn't wait to try it.

The next morning, I dropped
a toad into Bob's tank.
It wasn't as disgusting as I hoped.
Just one big gulp and Bob was done.
"Bummer," I said.

For the rest of the week,

Mr. Cooper let the class

bring in pets for show-and-tell.

Neil brought his ferret, Mr. Wiggles,

who wet all over the floor.

We had to leave the classroom

while it got cleaned up.

It was great!

On Thursday, Ryan brought in his skunk, Carl.

Carl cleared out *the whole school!*

I wish I'd thought of a skunk for a class pet.

I had to admit, Carl was cooler than Bob.

I was still thinking about Bob
the next day.

When was the last time I gave
him any toads?

Let's see, this was Friday.

I fed him on . . . Tuesday?

Oops!

"ARF! ARF! ARF!"

Just then, Andrea pranced in

with a prissy little poodle.

"This is Cupcake!

Isn't she sweet?"

Cupcake jumped out of
Andrea's arms and ran over
to Bob's tank.
She put her face right up
against the glass.
"ARF! ARF! ARF!"

"Back off, Cupcake!" I said.
I got over there just in time
to see Bob keel over!
He was lying on his back.
His little tongue was hanging
out of his mouth.

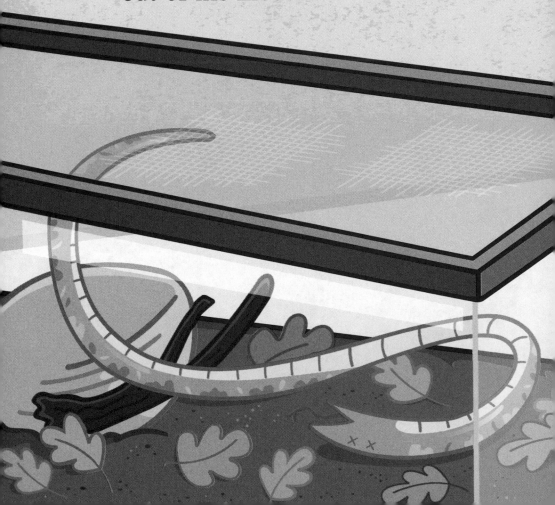

Oh my gosh.

BOB WAS DEAD!

"Andrea's dog killed Bob!"
A.J. shouted.
"Cupcake gave him a heart attack!"

"We've got to *do* something!"
yelled Emily, running out of
the room.

"Kids, calm down!"

said Mr. Cooper.

But everyone was busy freaking out.

I was freaking out the most.

Because I was pretty sure

I knew who *really* killed Bob.

"STOP!" I cried.

"It's my fault! I forgot to feed him!

He hasn't had any toads since Tuesday!"

"Alexia, he wasn't *supposed*

to have any more toads,"

said Mr. Cooper.

"He only eats once a week.

Remember?"

"Wait, you mean I *didn't* kill Bob?"

I asked.

A.J. started yelling again.

"I knew it was that dumb dog.

This is all Andrea's fault!"

Andrea looked like she was going to cry.

"I'm sorry," she said.

"I'll take Bob home and bury him."

She reached into Bob's tank

and picked him up.

Suddenly, Bob sprang to life!

"EEEEEEEEEEEEEEEK!"

shrieked Andrea.

Her mouth opened so wide

I saw her tonsils.

"Did NONE of you listen when
I talked about hognose snakes?"
cried Mr. Cooper.
"They play dead when they're scared,
like possums.
Bob is fine!"

Bob *is* fine. More than fine.

He's the best, coolest

class pet in the world.

Why?

Because Andrea HATES HIS GUTS.

Will Andrea learn to like Bob?

Will we ever let her forget about

shrieking her head off in class?

Will we trade Bob

for a fluffy little bunny?

Not on your life!